Praise for
SMOOCH'S WORLD

"*Smooch's World* by Kristan Shimpi is a touching tale of a lovable, clever, untrainable bullmastiff who instantly wins the hearts of her family. As mischievous and challenging as Smooch can be, she provides entertainment as well as comfort in times of need. I highly recommend this book to all animal lovers."

—Martha L. Thompson, Author of
*Giving Paws: Having a Service Dog
for a Hidden Disability*

"Meet Smooch—an oversized goofball with an oversized tongue who loves to smooch all she meets. Kristan Shimpi documents her family's hilarious seven-year love affair with a bullmastiff named Smooch, and it's a story that will appeal to anyone who has ever fallen in love with a lovable, high-maintenance fur ball with a huge personality! This is a feel-good book that is also smart, funny, and touching."

—Reba Hilbert, Editor of Dog Ear Publishing

"I loved this book! I curled up the night it arrived and just wanted to take a quick look. Well, a couple of hours later, I realized I never got up! It is a great book for all ages. I loved that you saw a picture after some of the chapters. You could use your imagination, then turn the page, and yep, my imagination was right on target with the picture. My daughter is now reading it. She was excited to come home and see that I had it ready for her to start. Thank you for allowing us to see a glimpse of Smooch's amazing life! You can tell Smooch loved her family, and she was definitely well-loved!"

—Sabrina Evans, Lover of All the Special Dogs

"This book was lovely. The chapters are quick, like small, delicious snacks that can be consumed in a sitting. Smooch was a rare beastie with no malice in her heart. She was huge and easy to love but seemingly not so easy to live with, and that made for many great stories. A fun read with some smiling tears at the end."

—Katherine Brown, Dog Owner

SMOOCH'S WORLD

(We Just Lived in It)

Smooch's World
(We Just Lived in It)
by Kristan Shimpi

© Copyright 2024 Kristan Shimpi

ISBN 979-8-88824-358-9

All rights reserved. No part of this publication may be reproduced, stored in a retrieval system, or transmitted in any form or by any means—electronic, mechanical, photocopy, recording, or any other—except for brief quotations in printed reviews, without the prior written permission of the author.

Published by

köehlerbooks™

3705 Shore Drive
Virginia Beach, VA 23455
800-435-4811
www.koehlerbooks.com

SMOOCH'S WORLD
We Just Lived in It

KRISTAN SHIMPI

VIRGINIA BEACH
CAPE CHARLES

TABLE OF CONTENTS

INTRODUCTION	1
WELCOME TO THE FAMILY	4
A WELL-TRAINED DOG	7
CHEWY, CHEWY	9
KICKED OUT	13
THE ONE EFFECTIVE TRAINING TECHNIQUE	15
THE GOOD COMMUNICATOR	17
PUPPY BOOT CAMP	21
SMELLY SMOOCH	24
THE DOG PARK	27
COMPANION CAMP	29
NAPPING EXPERT	32
EXERCISE . . . NOT A FAN	35
DISAPPEARING FOOD	39
ZOMBIE DAD	42
HOLIDAY SMOOCH	44
GREETING THE FAMILY	47
GRIEF SUPPORT	49
THE BASKETBALL FAN	51
CAT LOVER	54
SMOOCH THE CAMPER	57
LAKE LIFE	60
HOME WATER LIFE	65
THE CHICKEN MASSACRE	68
THE BOOK DEAL	70
SMOOCH THE GARDENER	73
PEDI-PEDIS	76
SPECIAL SLEEPING ARRANGEMENT	77
MY LAST TIME WITH SMOOCH	80
THE NEW NORMAL	83

CHAPTER 1
Introduction

In 2013, I turned forty. I was a parent of two school-age children, and my husband and I were trying to decide whether our family was complete. We could never get on the same page about more children. I would be ready, and he would be on the fence. Then he would be ready, and I would be unsure. One thing we did agree on was that we both needed to be on board. After all, with a third child, we would officially be outnumbered.

Even though we could not decide on more children, I had a strong desire to nurture. So, in a six-month time span, I collected four chickens, two cats, and a puppy named Smooch. Her name was pretty self-explanatory. Her tongue was so big that it did not fit into her mouth, and she used that tongue to smooch everyone she met.

We learned about Smooch from some friends whose children played travel soccer with our son. Like most families, you end up befriending and hanging out with families whose children participate in the same extracurricular activities. This family had us over for dinner one night, and we met Cooper—a giant bullmastiff and the most well-behaved dog I had ever met. I left that dinner knowing we would get a bullmastiff. A perfectly well-behaved dog.

My wish was set to come true without me doing anything about it. Cooper's mom made it her mission to get us a bullmastiff puppy and reached out to the folks she got Cooper from on our behalf. She also texted me multiple times a day with adorable pictures of Cooper. Seeing all of those adorable pictures *really* made me want a puppy. Luckily, one of Cooper's littermates had a litter of puppies, and there was one puppy left. There was someone interested in this puppy, but our family was chosen instead because we were friends with Cooper's family. Cooper's mom's wish was coming true. We would be getting that last puppy, a puppy named Smooch. That name cracked me up. *What kind of name is Smooch?* What a strange name for a dog. I would learn how appropriate that name was for our girl very soon.

Before I get into the story of Smooch and her life with our family, I should share that my husband was very reluctant to get a puppy. We had dogs in the past, and they were a lot of work. Plus, we already had the chickens and kittens from my fortieth birthday need-to-nurture. Add to this the fact that my husband grew up in a home without one pet—ever. Not even a fish. His mother was a pathologist by training, so animals meant germs and diseases. Why would you invite those gross things into your house? Despite his pet-less childhood, he was tolerant of our home becoming somewhat of a farm. That, my friend, is true love.

CHAPTER 2
Welcome to the Family

I WILL ALWAYS remember the day we drove to meet Smooch. My daughter skipped school to go with me (she had a cough, so missing school was semi-acceptable, even though the cough was most likely spring allergies). We headed to PetSmart to pick up some puppy supplies. I did not tell my husband we were getting a puppy, thinking it would be better to ask for forgiveness after he met Smooch and was instantly in love with her. This was a strategy I used a lot in our marriage, so it is actually surprising that we are still, in fact, married. He is no dummy, though. He had gotten the robot call saying our third grader was not in school that day. He called to ask why. After a long pause, he said, "You are going to get that puppy, aren't you?" My daughter and I giggled with delight, hoping our excitement would transfer to him. He didn't say *not* to go, which we both interpreted as him being totally on board.

We headed to Charlotte, North Carolina, to meet the transport person halfway from each of our homes. We smartly stopped at the local McDonald's for a quick lunch first. It had been a while since I had parented a puppy, but I did remember how impulsive they could be, especially around food. We gulped down some greasy cheeseburgers and fries and made our way to the gas station meeting point. I spotted Smooch right away. She looked almost regal sitting so nicely in the gas station grass. I decided right then that she was perfect, and I could not wait to get a smooch from her. We exchanged greetings and learned that Smooch had eaten breakfast and had her morning poop, so we should be good for the two-hour drive home. Wow, this was going to be such an easy transition. Boy, was I wrong!

The first thing Smooch did after licking my daughter's face and entire body was make a giant, stinky poop right in the back seat of the car. So much for that morning poop. We were already on the highway heading back home, so I pulled off at a truck stop to clean her up. She, of course, stepped in her very stinky poop and tried to eat it (a first sign of one of her most annoying habits). I only had a few hand wipes, and it was almost impossible to control my gag reflex while getting the poop off the car seats, Smooch, and my daughter, who, by the way, thought the whole scenario was hilarious. I got some truck stop toilet paper for the final cleanup, and we got back on the road home. That first experience gave me a small glimpse into our crazy future together.

CHAPTER 3
A Well-Trained Dog

We wanted Smooch to be a well-trained dog. This was a specific request of my son. Our previous dogs, while loved dearly, were not well trained. Smooch was definitely going to be different. The first step was to hire a trainer. We had four lessons from a trainer who came recommended by Cooper's mom. We had our treats and were ready to follow the trainer's directions exactly.

My daughter was very interested in the training process. For her science fair project the year before, she had actually clicker-trained our cat Fireball (a fluffy, orange Maine coon mix) to come on command and ring a bell. That project will always be near and dear to my heart. She was fascinated that you could give a command and a click, and the cat would do exactly what was asked. I did not have the heart to tell her that operant conditioning would work on any animal. I let her live in her training glory. She was so proud of her work, and to this day, if she says, "Fireball, come," the cat will appear within seconds.

She was ready to use her clicker training skills on Smooch, and after the first session with the trainer, she found a fanny pack to put around her waist to hold treats, just like the trainer did during our training session. She was all in, that is, until she realized that training a cat was a lot easier than training Smooch. The clicker and treats were not as powerful motivators for Smooch.

The first behavior that we wanted to extinguish was poop-eating. Yes, our dog named Smooch, who wanted to smooch everyone she met, ate her own poop. There are supplements that make poop not tasty to eat. What a strange concept since I thought poop would naturally not be tasty. We tried two different types of supplements to address coprophagia, the technical name for poop-eating. Neither worked. So, in the end, we did what we did for most of Smooch's undesirable behaviors; we modified her environment. This is a fancy way of saying we would run to scoop up the massive amount of poop she produced before she had a chance to snack on it. According to the American Kennel Club, 16 percent of dogs are classified as serious stool eaters. We knew Smooch would be special, but this was not what we anticipated.

Another behavior we focused on was walking on a leash. This behavior turned out to be rather easy to teach. Smooch would not tug to go faster, which was a good thing since she was growing rapidly. I think we went through four collars and harnesses in that first year. I loved watching Smooch walk with my daughter, who was eight years old when Smooch joined our family. She was extra careful when my daughter walked her. It was as if Smooch knew that she was small and could be knocked down if she pulled too hard.

The third behavior we focused on was a command. When Smooch engaged in an undesirable behavior, we called out, "Leave it!" For instance, when she tried to get into the kitchen trash can, we'd say, "Leave it!" When she jumped onto the counter to get food, "Leave it!" When she chased the cats, "Leave it!" When she chewed on things that she was not supposed to chew on, "Leave it!" Smooch would actually pause, but only for a second, then resume the undesirable behavior. Trained? Well, not so much. My husband graciously said that our family only liked dogs with "personality." I think that is actually a nice way of saying high maintenance.

CHAPTER 4
Chewy, Chewy

CHEWING WAS ONE of the biggest issues we had to deal with well beyond the puppy years. Smooch was the most oral dog I have ever known. And her giant mouth and teeth could demolish a dog toy in minutes. Even the toys that boasted they were indestructible. Nothing was safe. We tried giving her appropriate things to chew on, but she really preferred shoes and walls.

Our living room has a family tree sticker along the back wall, which most people think we put up as a decoration to complement our wall of family photos, but in reality, it was to cover all the places Smooch ate holes in the wall. I will always be grateful for the artists at Pottery Barn who came up with this brilliant decorating idea, even though our use of this art was not the intended purpose. What is the saying? Art is art . . . or art is in the eye of the beholder? Whatever the saying, the stickers saved our walls.

When Smooch was a puppy, someone was required to have a visual on her at all times. I put my husband in charge one Saturday when I was helping a friend with an estate sale. While he was "watching" her, she ate a hole in the living room wall. I was furious and questioned his supervision skills. Fast-forward two weeks later, and the same thing happened while I was "watching" Smooch. I am not sure who likes to say "I told you so" more in our family, but that phrase was used smugly when my husband found out about my supervision skills.

With two teenagers, retainers and removable braces (where were those fancy things when I was a teenager?) were constantly in and out of mouths. It turns out that a retainer was the perfect chew toy for Smooch—plastic and metal and something she could easily eat. My daughter had already lost her bottom retainer at school the first week after her braces came off, so imagine her frustration when she discovered Smooch had eaten the top one when she took it out to eat lunch. She was mad and blamed the dog until I reminded her that she had lived with the dog for quite a while and knew better than to leave anything on the table that Smooch could put in her mouth. I made her call the orthodontist to report that she not only needed a bottom retainer replacement but also a top one. In addition, we set up a payment plan for the new retainers. She also had to write not one but two entries in the book of shame at the orthodontist's office. I read the entries occasionally while waiting for one of the many follow-up appointments for all those retainers and braces. For every lost retainer or removable braces, the owner had to write how they lost said item and how they were going to pay restitution. I imagine the husband-and-wife team reading those entries over a glass of wine after work each evening and chuckling at the families.

Smooch's favorite toy was a musical mouse that we found at the local grocery store. It played this silly song we called "Bitley Be" when you squeezed it. Now, we have already established that Smooch could destroy even an indestructible chew toy in minutes, but she was very careful with her musical mouse. She would squeeze it ever so gently so it would play its song, and she would shake her head as if dancing to the music. The musical mouse toy lasted longer than any other, but only because Smooch wanted it to.

Even things you would not think would be appealing to eat fell victim to Smooch's giant mouth. For almost seven years, I kept my glasses on the coffee table when I would sleep with Smooch (more on this in chapter 28). One morning, I reached for my glasses on the coffee table, and nothing was there. I had to go to the bathroom to put in my contacts so I could look for them. When I came back to the couch, I found them half-eaten and buried in the blanket Smooch slept on. Thankfully, this happened in January, and I had an eye exam the prior month. So, I used my 2018 benefits for new contacts and my 2019 benefits for new glasses. And yes, I purchased the extra damage insurance in case Smooch decided these new glasses were a fun new chew toy as well.

The most stealthy of all stealthy chewing events happened on the way to one of our first lake trips. Smooch was sleeping on the floor of the car. Well, we thought she was sleeping. Apparently, while curled up into a tiny ball under my son's feet, she was very quietly chewing the leather side door cover. He swore he was "watching" her and could not figure out how she ate the door cover with him next to her. When I sold that car years later, it was very embarrassing to explain why the door cover looked the way it did.

Smooch was sneaky with her chewing habit, even when she was being carefully watched, as we all learned over the years. Because of this destructive habit, she was never left alone at home without her trusty crate to keep her mouth safe from everything she could find. I am scared to add up the total cost of her chewing addiction, but I know it was in the thousands of dollars.

CHAPTER 5
Kicked Out

THE FIRST SUMMER with Smooch in the family presented a problem we had not experienced before. Who would take care of her while we were at the beach for our annual Father's Day trip? I knew that we could not leave her at home and have someone check on her twice a day, which is what we had always done in the past with other dogs. Smooch needed way more attention. I cannot imagine what our home would have looked like with that plan in place. I do know what the house could look like while someone was "watching" her, so it would have been a scene from a horror movie if she were left alone for a significant amount of time.

My kids were doing a year-round swim team that summer, and I met another mom who was a pet sitter. She was trained as a physician but not practicing. She was a very strange person —a large German lady who was *very* opinionated. She asked to meet Smooch at our house, which seemed a bit odd, but I thought this must be how it works when you use a pet sitter.

Smooch was on her best behavior, mostly because I ensured she had a lot of exercise earlier that day. The pet sitter hung out with Smooch, and I walked her through Smooch's daily routine, the amount of food she ate, and her medications for the latest urinary tract infection. While the pet sitter was at our house, she commented about my husband and Smooch and how she could tell right away that he did not like the dog. I was surprised by her observations since my husband had been super tolerant of Smooch and all of her behaviors. My husband was pissed off. Why would a stranger come into our house and comment about *his* behavior? She was supposed to be observing the dog, not him. This was not turning out to be such a great idea, but our beach plans had been booked back in January when the idea of a puppy was nonexistent.

The Saturday before Father's Day, I dropped Smooch off with her toys, crate, blankets, and food. It felt like I had toddlers again. I got a quick smooch and left my mobile number for the pet sitter in case she needed to get in touch with me.

The dog sitter had older dogs that wanted nothing to do with Smooch, which did not seem like a concern to me. What I was concerned about was the fact that Smooch was still having accidents in the house. And as if on cue, Smooch squatted and peed as soon as she entered the house, of course, on the fancy hardwood floors of the living room. I explained that we were teaching her how to ring a bell to let us know she needed to go out, and the dog sitter quickly added, "There will be no time for that kind of training with the other dogs here." *Alrighty then*, I thought. So much for the training we had started at home.

The pet sitter texted me multiple times daily, complaining about Smooch's behavior. She even sent me pictures of the older dogs hiding from Smooch. I repeatedly apologized for Smooch's behavior but was not about to cut the vacation short to make her life easier. And we were paying for the service. When I picked Smooch up the following Saturday, she curtly said that it did not seem like a good fit for Smooch to come back. Getting kicked out of the pet sitter's house was probably the best thing that happened to us. The next boarding place we tried was Smooch's happy place, and it came with owners and staff who loved her almost as much as we did.

CHAPTER 6
The One Effective Training Technique

THE ONE TRAINING technique that did work with Smooch was the Invisible Fence correction system. We also had a seven-foot privacy fence in our backyard that we used for containment when we were not home. The Invisible Fence allowed our dogs to not only enjoy the one acre of woods in front of our property but also stay safe from the main road that had increasingly more traffic with new neighborhoods being built. Since we already had an Invisible Fence installed for our other dog, George, the basset hound, we had someone from the company come and train Smooch on the system. To our surprise, she needed a much smaller correction than our George. That little buzz was a real deterrent for big Smooch. Since this intervention was really all we had that worked, we used every single system the company provided. To keep Smooch from eating our shoes, getting in the trash, and trying to befriend cats that just wanted a safe place, we used a correction disk and flag.

I never once felt like this type of training was in any way cruel to any of our dogs. Smooch understood the system and respected the rules. I think I replaced her collar battery maybe twice in her entire life. Why? Because she rarely actually needed the correction. She just needed to understand the boundaries of where she could and could not go. I know this type of training method is controversial in the dog world. I also know that some trainers use it to dominate dogs and teach them to always submit to their leader. This was not our experience with Smooch, and we would never participate in those dominating ways of dog training. Smooch needed to understand that the correction was an option, but she always behaved in a way that made it unnecessary. I think of it like 1-2-3 Magic training for toddlers. When the toddler demonstrates an undesirable behavior, you count to one. If the behavior continues, you count to two. If you count to three, the toddler gets a time-out in minutes equivalent to their age. So, a toddler who is three years old gets a three-minute time-out. My oldest child would always make me count to two but never to three, which meant a time-out. Smooch was the same way with never needing a correction.

But all this training was starting to wear on the family. Especially me, since there was a phrase repeated by family members frequently: "You were the one who wanted the dog, so it's your problem." The most frustrating part was that we were so consistent with her training. Smooch just did not want to be trained.

CHAPTER 7
The Good Communicator

IN ADDITION TO training difficulties, Smooch had frequent urinary tract infections (UTIs) due to a hooded vulva. I can still remember my husband muttering, "Of course, only our family would end up with a dog with a hooded vulva." You might be thinking, *What exactly is a hooded vulva?* It is when there is a flap under the vulva, so when the dog pees, some of the urine gets trapped in the flap, which leads to infections. It took four different UTIs before our vet was able to find the right type of antibiotic that would work for Smooch. And in true Smooch fashion, it was an antibiotic not typically used to treat UTIs.

Barking was not in Smooch's repertoire, so we needed to figure out another way for her to communicate her frequent bathroom needs. I looked into having a dog door installed, but there was not an area big enough to make a door for a dog predicted to reach 120 pounds. Even if we had the space, making an opening that large would most definitely invite unwanted wildlife into our house. Our trainer recommended teaching Smooch to ring a bell to let us know she needed to go outside. This was one skill that Smooch *overlearned*. I lost count of how many work video conference calls included the ding of the bell, with me ejecting out of my seat to open the door for her. It turns out that I was very trainable.

Sometimes, Smooch would ring the bell and then decide not to go outside. This happened when it rained or snowed. She would ring the bell, I would open the door, and she would stare outside and let out a big sigh. The big girl did not like being cold or getting her feet wet. Often, if the weather at the back door did not meet her needs, she would try the front door, as if a different door might produce different weather.

Sometimes, Smooch would ring the bell with great frequency. This happened when my husband would smoke any type of meat on the Big Green Egg. For those unfamiliar with this type of cooking method, you slow-cook meat for eight to ten hours, and you need to check the temperature every fifteen minutes. My husband would go outside to check the temperature, and Smooch would head to the door and ring the bell so she could join him. Every fifteen minutes. For eight to ten hours. We nicknamed Smooch my husband's cooking assistant. She took her role very seriously.

While Smooch was not able to communicate with words, she did an excellent job letting us know what she needed. We just had to learn her code. Smooch preferred drinking water from a toilet bowl instead of a dog bowl. When she would drink the bowl dry, she would slam the lid down with her nose to indicate we needed to come and flush a fresh bowl for her. Before readers think our family is super gross, I should probably explain that this was what we called an "extra toilet." A building contractor convinced me to put it in when we added the mudroom to our house with the home addition. With this room, kids could come in and out to use the bathroom from the pool. That sounded like a great idea in theory, but it meant no one really used that toilet for its intended purpose. Hence, it became Smooch's water bowl.

When Smooch wanted her food bowl to be refilled, she would knock the bowl over with her nose to show there was no food in it. If that did not work, she knocked the lid off the basket of pool towels that was next to her food bowl. She wanted what she wanted when she wanted it.

One day, I was washing dishes, and the water slowed and then completely stopped coming out of the faucet. I immediately texted our plumber, and he came over to take a look. He came out from under the house where the well holding tank is and said, "I have never seen anything like that in twenty years of plumbing. The entire holding tank is empty, but that is not supposed to happen. You will need to call the water specialists since this problem is above my pay grade." Later that day, the water specialists came over and asked where water was leaking from in the house. I could not think of a place, so we had to pinpoint the location from under the house and then match that area inside. It was Smooch's toilet bowl. Apparently, that toilet had been continually running and refilling as Smooch drank the water from it. I actually liked this setup since it meant I did not have to constantly re-flush new bowls for her. Water mystery solved, a plumbing first for our experienced plumber, and back to flushing fresh bowls for my giant girl.

While Smooch never actually talked to me, we had conversations all the time. I worked in various roles at a local Girl Scouts club. And the drama was around every single corner you looked. Drama during cookie season (among adults, not the girls). Drama about volunteer roles and responsibilities. I would often talk to Smooch during and after meetings, sharing my honest thoughts about what was discussed. She was always on my side, of course.

Smooch was a persistent communicator for human food. Most people call this begging. She was excellent at smooshing her head under your arm, staring at you with those big brown eyes, as if saying, "I am starving to death. Please share your food with me." My husband would pretend to accidentally drop food (I guess that made him feel less guilty about giving in to Smooch) and say, "Whoops." Smooch learned quickly that "Whoops" meant something tasty was coming her way. My children did not participate in this game and said my husband and I were suckers for Smooch's antics. I am pretty sure they were correct.

CHAPTER 8
Puppy Boot Camp

WITH ALL THE health and behavioral issues, I was getting really frustrated with my Smooch. One day, while I was cleaning up one of her accidents inside, I saw her happily taking off all the lawn irrigation covers in the backyard. That was it. I was done with the dog, but I could not bring myself to re-home her. We have a motto: "Once in the family, always in the family." Both of my children were adopted, so I tried to imagine how they would feel if we got rid of Smooch because she was too much work. Plus, was I really going to let this puppy that was supposed to be so easy to train break me? Instead of re-homing Smooch, we sent her to puppy boot camp—a three-week stay that was supposed to fix any bad behaviors, guaranteed.

The phone conversation with the boot camp lady was exactly what I needed. She assured me that Smooch's annoying behaviors would be easily corrected. She had seen much worse with other dogs. Smooch just needed to learn who was in charge, and she could help us with that for a not-so-small fee. Feeling confident this was the solution we needed, we loaded Smooch up in the car the following week and headed to puppy boot camp.

Our first mistake was being late. The directions were unclear, and I did not have cell phone reception in the rural area. I ended up rolling down my car window and asking a man working in his yard if he knew how to get to the dog boot camp close by. He gave me directions in a way that felt like he had done that very thing many times before.

When we pulled up to the house, I noticed a tent-like structure in the front yard. From it stood a woman yelling at our car. "You are late. I explicitly said *not* to be late! I am working with another family now. You will have to wait." So that is what we did. We walked around the yard, waiting for our turn in the tent, wondering if this was a good idea after all.

While we were waiting, my son had to go to the bathroom. When I asked if he could go inside the house to use the bathroom, the puppy boot camp lady said he could go in the woods because guests were not allowed inside the house. This was not turning out to be the experience I was hoping it would be.

When it was our turn in the tent, the puppy boot camp lady asked about the behaviors we wanted to extinguish. I had my top three immediately: 1) stop eating her poop, 2) stop chasing the cats, and 3) stop chewing everything she could find. As I was listing off Smooch's undesirable behaviors, my son moved away from Smooch when she tried to lick him. Puppy boot camp lady said, "Don't do that. Show her you are in charge." He replied, "Okay, I am really not a dog person. I prefer cats because they are more predictable." Puppy boot camp lady responded, "Well, then, I feel sorry for you if you prefer cats. They are pure evil, I tell ya."

Then she explained that the behaviors we were concerned about were all very normal and could be fixed during the three-week stay at boot camp. She seemed really confident, but I was more reluctant. The living arrangements for the dogs at boot camp were outside. Each dog had an individually fenced-in area with a concrete pad and doghouse. There was a common area where the dogs could play together and work on skills. But I kept wondering how Smooch would work on the behaviors we were concerned about in this setting. For example, how could she learn not to chase cats if no cats were around? My hope was that if she learned anything at boot camp, it would be to stop eating her poop.

Reluctantly, we said goodbye to Smooch as the puppy boot camp lady assured us that our dog would still remember us when we returned in three weeks. She explained that dogs have no sense of time, which puzzled me a bit. One day is the same as one month or one year? That did not seem right to me, but I am also not an expert on dogs. As we drove out of the driveway, I almost turned around to say that we had changed our mind. But I also needed a puppy break, so we left our sweet, smart, and stubborn girl at boot camp to be reformed.

Three weeks later, Smooch came home still chewing on everything, chasing the cats, and, best of all, still eating her poop. A very important lesson was learned. If you want your dog to listen to you, do not let someone else train her with no follow-up to transfer those skills to you. Smooch learned to be an excellent listener to someone else and in a distraction-free environment. What we got was a very expensive vacation from our smart and stubborn puppy.

The UTIs resolved once we had Smooch spayed and paid the extra for a vulvoplasty to fix her hooded vulva, but the other behaviors remained. Modifying the environment remained our best weapon. And despite all her challenging behaviors, Smooch had a heart of gold. She simply loved just being with you. That was really what made her the happiest. And that damn tongue. When she would look at you with that tongue hanging out of her mouth and her head cocked to one side, it was hard to stay mad at her for very long.

CHAPTER 9
Smelly Smooch

THE FIRST SUMMER we had Smooch, we had a bad horsefly problem at our backyard pool. A friend suggested we get one of those hanging bug catchers that you fill with liquid that attracts the bugs and kills them once they drink it. The bug catcher worked really well, and after only a few days, it was full of dead bugs. While I was grateful for the flies to be contained, the bug catcher itself stunk. Knowing my mischievous puppy would be interested in this hanging toy, I made sure to hang it out of her reach. Or at least I thought I did. I came home from work one day to discover a wet and smelly Smooch, which meant an emergency dog grooming appointment. It took several washes to get the smell mostly gone. After paying that giant bill, I decided we would have to figure out how to coexist with the horseflies.

Smooch also liked houseflies. She would watch them buzz around her and then snap her giant mouth around them and eat them. I was always amazed at how fast she could move when she wanted to. Her favorite spot to catch flies was by the windows in the dining area. While catching her bug snack, she would leave tongue and nose smear marks on the windows. And best of all, sometimes, some actual bug guts would be left behind. The one bug she would not touch? The cockroach. I guess even Smooch knew they were nasty, disease-carrying insects.

In addition to bugs, Smooch had an obsession with squirrels. She chased them every chance she had. And one day, she finally caught one. No one really knows if she caught the squirrel or, more likely, found him dead. Regardless, she was proud of her accomplishment and carried that dead squirrel in her mouth for *hours*. No matter what we did to get her to drop it, she held on to it with fierce determination. I was impressed. Once she finally decided to drop it, there was coarse gray fur in her mouth that did not come off with regular drinks of water from her favorite water bowl. No one wanted the smell of dead squirrel fur as a part of her regular smooches. I am pretty sure there are some diseases associated with that kind of smooching.

Smooch was also smelly at times, which did not involve bugs or squirrels. She was a farter, one of the SBD kind (silent but deadly). Her farts could clear a room faster than you could say, "Smooch!" This behavior became a real issue when my children would have friends over. Do you preface a hang out with "just so you know, my dog farts, and they smell really bad. Like you might gag and want to throw up bad?" Or do you let the guests learn for themselves? Either way, it was super embarrassing for middle-school tweens.

CHAPTER 10
The Dog Park

THE TRAINER WE used to try to make Smooch the well-behaved dog suggested we socialize her early on since she would be a very large dog. We took this advice to heart and took her religiously to the local dog park. We, of course, visited the large dog section of the park.

Smooch loved going to the dog park, but as a puppy, she was unaware of her size. She would pounce on other dogs, just playing around, but some dogs were not a fan of Smooch's big love. She truly was not aware of how big her body was. Like a little child on the autism spectrum, Smooch would plow into another dog (or human) without any awareness. And how was I supposed to teach her body awareness? Most dogs would growl or show teeth to indicate they were done playing. That was our cue to put Smooch back on a leash and give the other dog a break.

The spring Smooch joined our family felt like monsoon season. It rained all the time. All day. All night. Every single day. At first, we stopped doing our outdoor activities because of the rain, but when it persisted for weeks and months, I decided we were just going to do what we normally would do. In the rain. This included going to the dog park. My kids would put on their raincoats and rubber boots. I would do the same and grab some towels for Smooch, and off we went. There were always a few other desperate-for-some-structure people there too, and our dogs would romp in the rain and mud and have a blast. I think this might have been the only time Smooch was okay with getting muddy. She liked clean fur and paws. I did cringe when she finished playing one afternoon and plopped right in a giant mud puddle to relax. Thankfully, her short fur was easy to clean off before getting back into the car.

Smooch made a friend at the dog park with an interesting habit she had never seen before. He would chase tennis balls that his owner launched into the air with this strange plastic throwing device. This dog was relentless. Over and over, he would chase the ball and bring it back to his owner. This friend was called a Labrador retriever, and this was considered their special talent. Smooch watched her friend retrieve that ball again and again and again.

There were all kinds of dog owners at the dog park—very social owners who wanted to chat with everyone they met, dog-obsessed owners who only wanted to talk about their dogs, antisocial ones, and the owners who let their dogs off-leash and played on their phones. It was one of these types of owners that ended our dog park fun.

One day, Smooch's play got to be too rough for a new friend, so we put her back on her leash. As did the other dog owner. But then, out of the blue, the other owner let his dog back off-leash, and the dog went straight for Smooch. I screamed and did exactly what you are *not* supposed to do during a dog fight. I screamed for my husband to intervene. He did, and Smooch bit him through the leg of his shorts. The kids were crying, I was scared and mad at the other dog owner, who should have never let his dog back off-leash, and my husband was hurt to the point of considering going to the ER. He ended up cleaning the wound thoroughly and was grateful for the thick fabric of his cargo shorts.

After a quick call to the trainer, I reassured the kids (and my husband) that Smooch acted on instinct, and we were the ones at fault for intervening. Lesson learned about dog parks. You might have control over your dog's behavior, but you cannot control the behavior of other dog owners.

CHAPTER 11
Companion Camp

After the dog park fail, we decided to find another outlet for Smooch to hang out with other dogs. A mutual friend told me about Companion Camp and said they offered day camp options. Fingers crossed they would accept my smart, stubborn big girl, I set up a time to visit. The owners, who were in the process of selling the camp to new people, adored Smooch. One of them even helped me troubleshoot some of Smooch's UTI issues. With Smooch, nothing was easy and straightforward. She always kept us thinking and on our toes. Day camp was perfect. Smooch got to socialize with other dogs, which did not result in an owner being bitten, and they tolerated all her special behaviors. Oh, and she did not get kicked out like at the first boarding place we tried.

The new owners loved Smooch even more than the original owners (if that was possible). Every single time I brought Smooch to camp, the staff would squat down and let Smooch *smooch* them all over. Smooch owned Companion Camp, and in her early years, she needed a lot of extra attention. At camp, each dog had their own cabin. Smooch was not a fan of the cabin dog door, which, by the way, kept the air-conditioning in the cabin. Yes, we boarded our dog in a camp cabin that had AC. Smooch would knock the cabin door off so she could see what was going on around her. She was also especially chewy at camp. At night, when she was alone, she would chew the wall. After a week at camp, the entire back wall would need to be re-drywalled. The staff at Companion Camp never complained about Smooch. They truly loved our girl.

Smooch had many boyfriends at Companion Camp. On each visit, she would pick out one male friend and give him all her attention. She pretty much owned the play yard too. In the summer months, there was a baby pool in the shape of a dog bone for dogs to cool off. When Smooch was in the play yard, she was the only one allowed in that pool. She would plop her giant body in it and refuse to get out until she was appropriately cooled off. I felt sorry for the other smaller dogs, who were probably just as hot as Smooch. No pool time for them until Smooch allowed.

We learned over time—and with lots and lots of drywall repair work—that giant deer jerky sticks helped keep the cabin drywall intact. At each drop-off, I would sign her in and grab one of the long deer jerky sticks that would be cut into smaller pieces and given to her each night of her stay. I am sure the staff was happy not to have to re-drywall her cabin wall after each of her stays. And as Smooch got older, she could play with more friends without the worry that she would push things too far in fun. I don't think she ever learned to share the baby pool, though. Sorry, other summer camp dogs, for my pool hog.

CHAPTER 12
Napping Expert

NAPPING WAS ONE of Smooch's specialties, and she preferred to nap on human furniture. No regular dog bed would do for Smooch. Like most other behaviors, we initially tried to restrict her from the furniture. To keep her off the fancy Restoration Hardware leather sofa, we used prickly pads that are placed on the cushions when not in use. I would wake up to find that Smooch had scooted the pads over each other, and she would be squeezed onto one of the cushions, happily snoring. How many dogs have their very own Restoration Hardware dog bed? Several visitors would glance at those prickly pads and ask what they were for. It was super embarrassing to say to keep the dog from getting on the couch. But our life was our life. Crazy and unexplainable and all that it was.

Smooch was not a quiet napper, snoring loudly when she was deep in sleep. We have many videos of Smooch happily sawing logs when she slept. You can always hear us trying not to laugh in those videos.

When Smooch was a puppy, a mortgage lender came to our house to help us sign paperwork to refinance our home. As we were sitting at the kitchen table signing paperwork that documented how we were never going to get out of paying the mortgage, I heard a strange sound. I looked around to determine where the sound was coming from and realized it was Smooch snoring. The mortgage lender could not stop laughing at our discovery. I am pretty sure we made his day—and possibly his week—with those lovely snoring sounds.

While napping, if Smooch thought I would make her get down from her sofa bed, she would curl herself into the smallest ball she could make, trying to make herself invisible. Super challenging for a 120-pound dog, but she tried anyway. And when it was time to get off her sofa bed, she did it very slowly . . . with a big sigh, stretching out her front legs, stretching out her back legs, then finally hopping down. Waking up was a process that could not be rushed.

Smooch had napping spots in all of her special places. She preferred her cooling cot on the back deck. In the front yard, she had one of the fire pit chairs. At the pool, she had a very specific chair that was hers. On our many lake trips, upon arrival, she would find the chair that would be hers for the weekend, and I placed the travel blanket on the special chair so it did not get drool or fur on it. Out of all her napping spots, however, her favorite was the Restoration Hardware couch, probably because it was the most expensive of her preferences.

CHAPTER 13
Exercise... Not a Fan

WHILE NAPPING WAS a favorite activity of Smooch's, exercise was not. Don't get me wrong; Smooch always wanted to be where we were—but only on her own terms. On her first of many lake trips, we stayed at a house with over a hundred steps to get to the dock. She would happily trot down to the dock but refuse to make the trip back up. Thankfully, she was still under fifty pounds, so my husband carried her up all those steps. After all, it was Smooch's world. We just lived in it.

On an outing to explore the spring flowers at Duke Gardens, she decided the walk was done at the entrance to the garden on our way out. No encouragement or treats would change her mind. By then, she was well over a hundred pounds, so carrying her to the parking lot was not an option. Being a good sport, my husband got the car and drove us to Smooch so she could get in for her ride home. For someone who did not want another dog, he was often a good sport when dealing with Smooch's less-than-desirable behaviors.

The spring Smooch joined our family, I was a Girls on the Run (GOTR) coach. GOTR is a running program for elementary-age girls. Over a twelve-week period, girls learn how to run a 5K while also learning how to be strong and self-confident. Smooch came to the twice-weekly sessions and loved all the attention she got from the girls. But running, not interested at all. She would run one lap, then sit next to me while waiting for all fifteen girls to run by her and give her a scratch on her head. Smooch even came to the celebratory 5K race as our mascot, sporting a hot pink GOTR bandana made by the participating girls.

Smooch's longest exercise activity was a hike on the Virginia Creeper Trail. We camped with friends at the nearby state park for the weekend and decided to check out the very famous trail. I was a little nervous that Smooch would quit mid-hike, so I took some highly desirable treats to tempt her to keep going if she got tired. I also packed an extra water bottle and a handy travel bowl. We were having such a good time hiking and chatting that I did not even realize how far we had hiked on the trail. And the trail was an out-and-back, which meant that no matter how far we hiked, we had to go the same distance to get back to the car. As I was processing this realization, I noticed a seriously happy Smooch with a large smile around her giant tongue. It was a hot July summer day, so the trail was packed with hikers and bikers. Almost every single hiker stopped to pet Smooch and comment on how "handsome" she was . . . *hello, why did people not notice that her harness was pink?* When she saw the hikers, she would approach them, shaking her head from side to side, with her giant tongue hanging out, waiting for them to pet her. It was her expectation as if she was saying, "Hello, I am here, and I am super cute. Now you have to pet me." She loved the attention and slept like a champ at the campsite that night.

While Smooch was overall a pretty lazy girl, she would sometimes have sudden bursts of energy, running in a giant circle in the yard at high speeds and then going back to napping. I could never figure out the triggers that made her break out into a sprint. It just happened. And when friends were around, they would marvel at how fast she could move for such a big and lazy girl. Maybe those bursts of energy were Smooch's way of doing high-intensity interval training.

In Smooch's later years, the vet would weigh her at her checkups and ask me to restrict her snacking since she could no longer feel

Smooch's ribs during the physical exam. I would think to myself, *How do you restrict snacks and table food for a 120-pound stubborn lady?*

CHAPTER 14
Disappearing Food

EVERYONE IN OUR family learned early on to never, ever leave food on the kitchen counter, dinner table, or anywhere within Smooch's reach. Someone had to be in the kitchen or at the dinner table to yell, "Leave it!" while food was around. Sometimes, friends and relatives learned this lesson the hard way . . . with disappearing food. One minute, it was there; the next, it was gone.

Smooch was what you would call a counter surfer. Nothing was safe. We implemented strategies like pushing all food to the very back of the counter and placing things like trivets in front of the food to deter Smooch, but she was stealthy and persistent. And she could stretch her body out long to try and reach the precious food she wanted.

So many food items were stolen and ended up in her mouth—a sandwich on the table while a visiting friend went into the kitchen for water, a turkey leg on the counter at Thanksgiving. That steal prompted some very funny *Christmas Story* jokes, like the Bumpus hounds that stole the Christmas turkey. "Watch my plate" became the mantra at our home.

When she wasn't stealing food at mealtimes, she preferred to sit with me while I ate. A giant Smooch squeezed behind me in my chair as I ate my dinner. I tried to ignore her, but she would lean around me, sigh, and give me a lick with that giant tongue. That was it. All I could do was laugh. And Smooch, more often than not, ended up with food treats as a result.

CHAPTER 15
Zombie Dad

My husband and I have always taken Halloween costumes very seriously. Some of my favorite couple costumes have been Eleven and Dustin from *Stranger Things*, Laurie Strode and Michael Myers from the *Halloween* movies, and best of all, Evil Kittie and Zombie Dad. That particular Halloween, we were attending a party at a friend's house in the neighborhood next to our house. The Zombie Dad costume was a zombie mask and business attire (button-down shirt, tie, and coat). For some reason, my husband decided to make everyone guess who he was at the party. *How?* you might be wondering. He did not speak to anyone. It was actually hilarious. Everyone at the party was trying to figure out who was Zombie Dad.

That mask was a huge issue with Smooch, which took us all by surprise. Smooch was not what you would call a guard dog. She loved everyone: friends, strangers, and potential enemies. I have so many memories of her sleeping in her crate or on her deck cot, legs sticking up in the air without a care in the world, even with total strangers doing work on our house. The doorbell never startled her. People coming and going to and from the house was never an issue. So, imagine our surprise when my husband donned his zombie mask, and Smooch charged at him like he was the most evil of all enemies. He quickly pulled the mask off as Smooch charged closer to him, and that was all it took to call off the attack. That mask did not appear on my husband's face inside our house ever again. Only a Halloween party favor from then on out. But it did make us realize that deep down inside our lovable, never-met-a-stranger dog was a true guard dog at heart.

CHAPTER 16
Holiday Smooch

WE TAKE HOLIDAY cards very seriously in our house. Well, I guess *I* take holiday cards very seriously. We always have really good ones, the kind that people comment about the entire month of December. Finding the perfect picture can take all year, but I always know when I have the right one.

I knew Smooch had to be on the holiday card in 2014, but how to get the best shot was the big question. One strategy I used was to look at the designs from some of my favorite online card sites and try to figure out what type of picture(s) I needed (landscape, horizontal, multiple shots, etc.). When I saw the "All Is Calmish and Bright" design on Minted.com, I knew the photo I needed. The design featured three children with the caption "All Calmish and Bright" below. What made the design super funny was that each child had a halo over their head. The child in the middle had a crooked halo, indicating why things were only calmish and not calm. Smooch would be our middle child.

I got the perfect shot of my three children, with Smooch and her giant tongue right in the middle, but it took a little work. I had Smooch jump on our bed (a prohibited spot, normally) with one child on each side of her. Then, I held down the camera button continually. Out of close to a hundred shots, I got the perfect one. I think I sent that card out the first week in December, and it was the talk of the month. People I had not heard from in years—but for some reason were still on our holiday mailing list—commented on the card. The orthodontist, who we really only saw at braces or retainer consultations, even came into the waiting room to tell me how much she liked the card. That holiday card will always be my favorite.

CHAPTER 17
Greeting the Family

Smooch loved her family, and she greeted each family member in a unique way. I think she knew who could tolerate her slobbery kisses better than others. She greeted my daughter with full gusto, running to greet her at the door with big tongue licks. She was more reserved with my son. He would often ask as he entered the house if Smooch had eaten her poop that day. This was his gauge as to how many tongue licks he was willing to allow. A fair assessment, I should add.

Smooch really loved my husband, though. How did I know? Every day when the husband came home from work, Smooch would somehow know it was him. Maybe because the rest of the family was home at that point. I don't know, but as soon as the lock would click, Smooch would trot to the door, shaking her head from side to side. She never jumped on him; instead, she waited patiently for him to scratch her on her head and tell her how much he missed her while he was at work. This happened every single day, and Smooch never greeted anyone else in such a special way. I think she knew how hard he worked and wanted to let him know how much she appreciated him.

With me, whenever I was not home, she was in her crate—her special cave of love with blankets and stuffed toys. When I came home, I greeted her with a high-pitched "I am home, sweet Smoochie," and she would lift up her back legs to stretch as she prepared for me to open the crate door. She exited the crate slowly, on her own terms, and gave me a good, long smooch to welcome me home. That girl really did just want to be with her family, so our special greetings were her way of saying she was happy to be back with us.

CHAPTER 18
Grief Support

In May of 2015, my mom died unexpectedly. She had been in bad health for a while, but it was still a shock when my brother called me that Wednesday morning to say he found her unconscious in her apartment. She had very specific DNR requests, but the hospital put her on a ventilator until both my brother and I could come and agree to have it removed. That was literally the hardest day of my life. I was angry her depression was never treated.

A similar scenario happened a year earlier. My brother and I found her living in trash, unable to breathe. Although we both agreed she needed to go to the hospital, we had very different opinions about everything else. I immediately contacted the hospital social worker and was told to document her current living arrangement with photos. That would be the type of information needed to prevent her from returning to those living conditions. My brother had a different plan. He hired a company to clean out the trash from the apartment so our mom could come back home. As I prepared to call the social worker, my mom said that if I made that call, she would never speak to me again. Sadly, she kept her promise, and that was the last conversation we ever had.

On that Wednesday in 2015, I sat outside of her hospital room, watching her heartbeat and breathing drop to dangerously low levels on the hospital monitors. After about an hour, I realized that I could not sit outside that room and listen to her die, so I said my goodbyes and left. Those sounds will haunt me forever. I will always regret that being my last memory of my mom.

As I tried to process my grief that summer, Smooch sat with me and watched our first bluebird family move into our backyard, which was totally unexpected. You see, my mom had tried to attract bluebirds to our house since I moved into the first version of our home in the mid-1990s. With no luck. She tried the correct type of house, facing the correct distance from the sun and the exact height, to entice them to make our home theirs. It never happened until the week after she died. And it turns out, they did not need the perfect house with all those special amenities. After the raccoons ate the suet out of the fancy suet feeder gifted to me by my mother-in-law, I replaced it with a generic birdhouse from Target simply meant to take the space of the high-cholesterol device I previously had up for the neighborhood raccoons. The week after my mom died, a bluebird family moved into that house. Now, I am not a very religious person, but I know with all my heart that it was my mom letting me know she was okay. Three broods of baby birds lived in that birdhouse that summer, and we watched them all fledge the nest while remembering my mom. My daughter, Smooch, and I sat on the pool deck at the end of that summer and watched the last bluebird brood fledge. I said that we had to let our sadness and anger over Nana's death go with those babies. We did our best to do just that.

I was a mess that summer. I did what was expected of me, but just the bare minimum. Through it all, Smooch was by my side, willing to listen to me cry even after others felt like it was time to move on. That big girl was a great listener, and she was always there when you needed her.

CHAPTER 19
The Basketball Fan

In our house, we are what is affectionately called a "house divided." Some family members cheer for one basketball team, while others cheer for another team. The girls are Carolina Tar Heel fans, and the guys are Duke Blue Devil fans. College basketball is a big deal where we live. People are diehard fans of their teams. As a girl, Smooch was rightly a Tar Heel fan.

My husband and I taught our children the rules of being loyal fans early into their toddler years. I would teach them to chant, "Go Heels!" He would teach them to chant, "Go Duke!" We realized that we needed to learn (or pretend) to be better sports for the kids' sake, but the rivalry ran deep within our family.

During tournament season, my daughter and I would participate in rituals to ensure the Tar Heels would win. In the first tournament season Smooch participated in, I dressed my daughter in the 2009 championship T-shirt and the 1993 championship hat and gave her a pom-pom from the 2005 championship. She let Smooch play with the pom-pom, which meant she ate it, so it should not have been a surprise when her poop had strands of white and light blue strings in it the next morning. The not-so-fun part of this Tar Heel loyalty? Using a paper towel to gently pull the strings from her bum.

One year during the ACC tournament, Duke had a hashtag #housedivided challenge on Instagram. I submitted family pics, including one of Smooch and her pom-pom. Imagine the surprise on my husband's face when our family was chosen for the Duke Daily Newsletter. He had fellow doctors, nurses, and even patients in the waiting areas of the hospital commenting on our house-divided family and super cute dog, despite her loyalty to the wrong team.

CHAPTER 20
Cat Lover

TWO CATS WERE already residents at our house before Smooch arrived. I researched how to introduce a puppy to cats and followed all the recommendations. We designated the upstairs as the cat-safe zone so Smooch could not find their food and litter box. I figured if she ate her own poop, she might also like cat poop. We put an Invisible Fence correction disk and flag at the bottom of the steps to remind her that she was not allowed in that area.

We had brief hangouts with all three of the family pets, and it was clear from the beginning that the cats were not fans of Smooch. She was still a puppy but already double their size. Smooch was also not aware of her size and had personal space issues. Our cat, Fireball, was especially distrustful of Smooch. At first, the cats ran from Smooch to a safe zone in the house; often, that was upstairs, but over the years, they became braver and stood up to Smooch more often. I have so many memories of the cats and Smooch—Fireball, hissing, with his back arched and paw out, ready to scratch Smooch. And Banjo (an orange and white standard domestic shorthair cat) with his ears flat against his head underneath the coffee table, safely out of reach from giant Smooch.

Over the years, the cats and Smooch learned to coexist. If Smooch was napping in the kitchen, they would very quietly sneak around her to get to where they wanted to go. Sometimes Smooch would wake up, but if she was having a good nap, she would most often give the cats a quick glance and then return to her snoozing.

Shockingly, Smooch was only scratched once by one of our cats. She was smart enough not to get too close. Fireball was the lucky cat who scored the scratch right on the tip of Smooch's nose. That scratch bled forever. My son was the one who witnessed the encounter. He screamed, "Smooch is bleeding, and there is so much blood. Come help me, Mom!" I raced to the kitchen. Fireball was on the counter. Smooch had a puddle of blood in front of her. I tried to wipe her nose to stop the bleeding, but Smooch had a super sensitive snout and was not a fan of people touching it. In the end, I just let her outside to take care of her injury by herself, which meant wiping her nose over and over in the grass. I thought that scratch would be the deterrent for Smooch—a signal that the cats had a powerful weapon they could use if she got into their space. Nope. Smooch was a cat chaser her entire life.

CHAPTER 21
Smooch the Camper

I AM NOT A camper, but when my son joined Cub Scouts in first grade and I realized everyone in my family except me liked to camp (my daughter also went on Cub Scout camping trips with other siblings and had a blast), I tried to figure out how to do it for my family. We ended up getting a pop-up camper, which felt like a good compromise. We could camp outside, but I would not have to sleep on the cold, hard ground. Oh, and our camper even had AC and a portable potty. I think the term for my type of camping is "glamping."

Smooch happily came along, but she had certain expectations. The camper folded out so that each side had two double-size platform beds. There was also a single bed that could serve as a couch or eating area in the middle. I slept with Smooch on one side while my husband and daughter slept on the other side. My always agreeable son slept on the single bed in the middle. Smooch loved this arrangement, but because she was sleeping somewhere different, she would wake up three or four times a night to survey her surroundings, give me a lick and sigh, readjust with her head on my belly, and fall back asleep. This might not sound like a big deal until you remember that I was sharing my sleeping space with a 120-pound dog. Her adjustments would literally shake the camper.

Smooch did not enjoy eating her dog food while camping. At mealtimes, we would have to put Smooch on a tie-out so she could not reach the picnic table. If she could, whatever was on it would be hers to eat. She got lots of human food while camping—the ends of hot dog buns, chips, and one of her favorite snacks . . . fruit.

Sounds in nature did not bother Smooch, so she was not at all phased when, during one night of camping, my daughter woke me up to say that something was outside of the camper. I fumbled around to find my glasses since I am legally blind without them and discovered a giant raccoon sitting on our picnic table with his paw literally inside a bag of chips. Just sitting there snacking on the food that my son left out on the table (a big camping no-no). My daughter whispered that it was Rory saying hello from one of our favorite books, *Furiously Happy*, and we watched as he finished off the bag, grabbed the veggie tray, and headed back into the woods.

We only lost Smooch once while camping. She never really left my side, so I was surprised when I came out of the camper one morning after getting my hiking boots, and she was nowhere to be seen. My kids hopped on their scooters and circled around the campground twice. No Smooch sightings. My husband and I went in opposite directions, looking for her and calling her name. After about thirty minutes of looking, convinced someone had kidnapped her, I found her sleeping on a blanket next to someone's early morning campfire, oblivious to our calls and worries and snoozing by the fire. I wonder what the campers would have thought if they had come out of their camper to find a giant beast by their campfire. Not everyone loves big dogs, so I am glad I found the sleeping giant before they did. From then on out, Smooch was on a tie-out if left solo, just in case she decided to explore again. Keep in mind—if she had just come when called (basic recall), something almost every dog does with one-hundred-percent accuracy, the whole situation could have been avoided.

CHAPTER 22
Lake Life

SMOOCH WAS HAPPY being with you, wherever you were, even if that was not at home. I have always been a lover of lakes, but this connection deepened after the unexpected death of my mother in the spring of 2015. I would take weekend trips during the nicer months of the year. My family deemed it "lake therapy" and knew that twenty-four hours next to water would be good for the whole family.

Smooch was my lake buddy, going on every single trip except for one. Upon arriving at the Vacation Rentals by Owner (VRBO) rental, she would establish which chair was hers, and then I would put a blanket on the selected seating so her loving slobber would not get on the furniture. She loved to go on the lake dock and take in the view. I would usually keep her harness on her, but not once did she leave the designated area. She really did only want to be where we were.

Lake trips meant time in the car. I knew from planning for life with a giant breed dog that we would need a reliable way to get her in and out of the car. I also knew that lifting her was not a good option since she was guaranteed to be over a hundred pounds. I got one of those fancy car ramps that you hook to the back of the car so Smooch could just walk up into the back of the car. It even had a rough section in the middle so she would not slide off. Our trainer said to introduce the ramp using treats. There were no treats tempting enough to get

Smooch on that ramp. I even tried dragging her onto it so she would see it was safe. Nope. That fancy ramp still lives in the workshop, gathering dust. We ended up putting Smooch in the back seat for trips. She would get her front legs into the car, and I would squat and lift her back legs in.

With Smooch in the back seat, it meant that one of the kids had to ride along with her. My son would always pick the front seat if he had a friend along, so additional passengers always sat in the back with Smooch. Well, it wasn't exactly Smooch sitting *with* you, more like sitting on top of you. Time in the car also meant we had to deal with Smooch's flatulence in close proximity. That girl was gassy. Road trips always included rolling down the windows to air out the car multiple times, depending on the length of the car ride.

Smooch was perplexed by the concept of fishing. I would attach a little wiggly thing on a hook, drop it in the water, and bam—a fish would come out of the water. I would take a picture of the fish and toss it back into the lake. Repeat ten to twenty times. Smooch would be interested in my catches initially but then stare at me as if saying, "You really think this is fun, strange lady?"

The kids had a lake routine as well. They would run into the VRBO to pick out which rooms they wanted. On one lake trip, my son and his friend grabbed the room with two bunk beds. This choice turned out poorly for him. The next morning, after probably going to bed around 5 a.m., he was sleeping on the bottom bunk, mouth wide open. Smooch went to him, doing what she did best . . . smooching him all over the face. I don't think my son will ever sleep on a bottom bunk ever again.

In the summer of 2016, I took my daughter and a friend to check out Lake Tillery. The house was next to the lake marina and was owned by the people who managed the marina. They offered us a good deal to take a pontoon boat out for a few hours on a slow boat rental day. Driving a boat had been on my life's bucket list for quite a while, so we all loaded up on the boat to check out the bigger parts of the lake.

Smooch sat at the head of the boat with the wind making her giant jowls flap in the wind. That was a great day for all of us.

In the winter of 2018, my daughter was struggling with anxiety and depression. I knew that the best defense would be a good offense, so I planned a weekend lake trip for her and a friend. I also wanted to have some one-on-one time to discuss what was bothering her and how I could best support her.

It was cold that weekend, and the lake was in the Tennessee mountains, so we woke up to a dusting of snow the second day. Smooch and I took a walk outside with my morning coffee. Because the house was pretty secluded, and Smooch always stayed close by, I let her off her leash to check out the dock. Imagine my surprise when I heard a loud splash, and when I turned around, there was no sign of Smooch. It took a few seconds to register that she had slipped on the icy dock and fallen into the cold lake. As I was processing it all, I started jogging toward the dock, taking off my glasses and putting down my phone so I could jump in to save my giant baby. But as I approached the dock, Smooch popped to the surface and dog paddled to the bank. She was not a happy dog, rubbing her short snout on the grass and trying desperately to shake off the cold water. Needless to say, she stayed clear of the dock for the rest of the trip. It was a lesson learned for me. A floating dock can dip down a bit with enough weight on it.

Our last lake trip was in February of 2019. We went to Mayo Lake, which is only a forty-five-minute drive from our house. I took my son and a friend along since the rental had a man cave for a basement—Foosball, Ping-Pong, lots of leather reclining seats, and a giant TV. The weather was not great, but Smooch was at my side while I recharged. I put together a puzzle, knitted, watched Netflix, and took in an amazing lake view despite the rain.

Since Smooch was a huge lover of lakes, I decided we should try a trip to the beach. I also wanted to check out Topsail Island since we always went to a neighboring beach for summer vacations. Top Sail is a fun place to visit, but you would never want to own something waterfront there. Hurricanes have eroded the beachfront to a tiny strip of sand. Most of the waterfront properties have steps that go right out to the water.

The weather was questionable, so the rest of the family bailed on the trip. It was just me and my Smooch. I stopped at the local grocery store to get food for the day and one of those fancy logs that can burn from the middle. After unpacking, Smooch and I camped out under the carport, watching the waves with our burning log. I saw a school of dolphins super close to shore. For me, that in and of itself justified the nearly three-hour drive to the beach.

Before the trip, I asked fellow dog owners about ocean water. I knew that dogs should not drink it, but I was also not sure how to enforce that rule. Dogs are either ocean drinkers or not. Fortunately, Smooch sniffed the salty water and wanted nothing to do with it. She was also not a fan of high tide. She got visibly irritated when the water washed up to her paws. With lake water, she was in control of when it touched her—not so much with ocean water. Smooch liked the seagulls, but unlike the chickens, they could fly away when she got too close.

We took long walks along the beach on that trip. She liked these walks as long as she was safely away from the moving water. Even though Smooch was not a beach girl, as always, she was happy just being wherever I was, even if that was at the beach.

CHAPTER 23
Home Water Life

Smooch loved our backyard pool, but not as a place to swim. We tried to get her to swim, but she would dog-paddle right back to the steps each time we tried to get her to come in. She did like to get in the water, though. She would climb down the first three steps, just deep enough to get her underbelly wet, drink some of the water, and then climb back out. When friends would come for pool hangouts, Smooch would walk around the edge of the pool and give smooches to anyone at the edge. She also liked to hang out on the lounge chairs. She claimed a very specific chair for herself, and if someone took her chair, Smooch would politely squeeze in and gently nudge the person off the chair. More often than not, guests would be sitting on towels while Smooch was in charge of her lounge chair. If a guest tried to share the chair with Smooch, she would stretch her giant body out so there was only room for her.

Because of Smooch's chewing habits, there were strict protocols for pool accessories. By this point, my children knew better than to leave nice plastic flip-flops or, even better, a pair of Crocs by their pool towels. I would collect all things that could be chewed, and they either went directly into the pool or in the workshop. It was embarrassing to admit these protocols, especially to new friends or people who weren't dog people, but it was our way of coexisting with Smooch.

In December of 2017, we decided to dig a pond in the woods in front of our house. It was a compromise of sorts. I had dreamed of owning a lake house for many years, but with two children in a super expensive private school, we could not justify the additional mortgage. The pond would be at-home lake therapy and a lot less expensive than a lake house.

The contractor who built the pond said it would fill naturally with rain and water runoff in three to four months. That winter was an especially wet one, so our pond was completely full in just a little over one month. After it filled, we added an aerator and fish. If you are wondering why the pond needed an aerator, which I did, here is the explanation. Most ponds have a natural water source—a stream, river, or creek. That natural water source provides the needed oxygen for the fish. Interesting, huh? Our pond would be filled with rain and runoff water, so we had to add oxygen to keep the fish healthy.

As the pond filled, the amphibians started to find our new body of water. They came out by the thousands. There were types of frogs and toads that I did not even know existed. Thank goodness for Google to help me identify all the new species. Smooch loved the frogs and toads. She would walk to the edge of the pond and jump when they plopped in the water at the sight of her big body. Smooch also liked to drink the pond water, and she had a very specific place she liked to drink from. I called it her personal water hole.

There is a bridge over one edge of the pond, and Smooch spent many afternoons napping there as I hung out with friends at the firepit. I think she preferred the bridge area since the smoke from the firepit made her sneeze. That bridge was her happy spot, and I hope I can always visualize her there, sunning herself and soaking up life.

CHAPTER 24
The Chicken Massacre

IN THE FALL of 2016, three years into life with backyard chickens, Smooch decided the Invisible Fence correction was no longer a deterrent. I had it set up so the chickens had their area, and an Invisible Fence kept Smooch out of that area. Apparently, the visual reminder was not enough to keep her from her feathery friends. Why, though, after living with them all of these years, I will always wonder.

Her first playdate happened while I was on a work phone call. She rang the bell to go out in the backyard. I was obviously distracted, so when she did not come right back to the door and my call was over, I looked for her. Smooch had cleared the Invisible Fence and was "playing" with one of the chickens. The chicken was still alive but a bit gimpy in the right leg. She still wanted to drink water, so I decided she might make it. I put her in the nesting box and knew that there would be one of two results in the morning—she would perk up or be dead.

I went to the chicken coop the next morning, and the chicken was dead in the nesting box. The kids were mad at Smooch, and I had to explain that some dogs have that need to chase and kill as a part of their innate disposition. Not even an Invisible Fence can correct for that 100 percent of the time. But it did mean we needed to be more aware when Smooch was in the backyard and not let it happen again.

Fast-forward two weeks later. One of our chickens kept leaving their fenced-off area. We were trying really hard to police Smooch from getting off the deck to go in their area, so it was not helpful that this one chicken decided to roam the whole backyard. That night, I put the roaming chicken back in her area and let Smooch out to pee. I thought the gate was secured, but apparently, Smooch opened the gate with her nose while we were watching TV and went for the chickens. After "playing" with the chickens, she brought one to the back door . . . almost, but not all the way, dead. Sigh. This time, I knew I had to do the humane kill and not wait until the morning. Thankfully, we had a sharp axe, and the whole process was quick. I went to put the other two chickens up and found them dead in their designated area. So, in mere minutes, Smooch had killed all our chickens.

The next morning, I went to the chicken coop to find only one dead chicken. Walking around clucking like normal was Godzilla. Apparently, she was playing dead in a corner of the fence. That and the fact that she had black feathers probably faked Smooch out the night before. You might be wondering why we had a female chicken named Godzilla. This should explain it—the ten-year-old son was in charge of naming her. Do I need to say more?

I very quickly decided that we needed to re-home Godzilla. That chicken had survived Chatham County coyotes and Smooch, but policing Smooch and her love of chicken toys was just too much. I posted on Facebook, and my daughter's preschool teacher offered to take Godzilla. What a relief. And wouldn't you know it . . . that chicken popped out an egg like she had done every single day since January of 2013, despite almost being killed the night before. We said farewell to Godzilla and hoped her new home had less excitement and lots of places to enjoy a dog-free life.

CHAPTER 25
The Book Deal

I AM WHAT you might call an amateur photographer. I love taking pictures of pretty much anything. This hobby led me to friendships with other like-minded people, so when a friend posted on Facebook that a fellow photographer was looking to do a photo shoot with a large dog and small child, I reached out to see if we were a good fit. My daughter was not exactly a small child, but Smooch was definitely a large dog. The photographer asked me to send a few pictures of Smooch, and once he saw that giant tongue, he agreed to do a photo shoot for us. It was a win-win situation. He got amazing pictures to use for his portfolio, and we got three digital images of our favorite photos.

The actual photo shoot was a cardiovascular experience for all involved. We would get Smooch ready to pose, and then she would get distracted and jump down. We used treats and spoke in high voices to try to get her back on the stage area, but it was constant up and down, up and down. All with that giant tongue panting away.

I loved watching my daughter with Smooch, but especially during that photoshoot. Despite her uncooperative behavior, the unconditional love in my daughter's eyes for her giant goofball of a dog was so apparent. We laughed the entire drive home about Smooch and the exhausting photoshoot and hoped the photographer got at least three good photos of her. After all, that was what we were promised for our time and the hard work involved. Smooch, having exerted all her physical activity for an entire week during the photo shoot, slept the entire way home.

A few weeks later, we got our three photographs, and they were amazing. You would never know how much effort it took to get those perfect shots. There was one, of course, of Smooch doing what she did best on my daughter's cheek.

A few years after the photo shoot, we heard from the photographer again. He had been diagnosed with a terminal illness, and he was making one last book before he died. It is titled *A Last Love Letter to My Friends: Celebrating Dogs and the Joy They Bring Us*. Smooch has three photos in that book. The best part is that the proceeds from book sales are donated to charities benefiting dogs. Dog lovers are good people. I am happy to have met Rick Fisher.

CHAPTER 26
Smooch the Gardener

WHEN WE HAD our backyard pool built in the summer of 2008, we had to build a retaining wall to make the area level. My daughter took three seed packets of annuals and spread them out in the dirt of the retaining wall. I used the flowers that sprouted that summer to teach her about how annuals can reseed themselves naturally with the seed pods. She popped every single seed pod with delight, watching the new seeds fall to the ground. As a result, by the time Smooch joined our family, we had a retaining wall overflowing with annuals. Smooch had a favorite—purple coneflowers. She would barrel into the flowers in the retaining wall, sit down (most of the time crushing the sedum and black-eyed susans), and munch on the purple coneflowers. A quick Google search told me why. Those flowers contain echinacea, which has health benefits like boosting the immune system, reducing bad breath, and alleviating physical discomfort. So, it looks like Smooch picked her favorite flower for a good reason.

I loved having potted plants on our back deck—close enough to water easily, and the deck area gets a good amount of sun, so lots of things would grow there. Smooch was not a fan of potted plants. If I put out a potted plant on the deck, she would wait until she was outside alone and dump the contents of the pot out, take the pot in her mouth, and run gleefully around the backyard. We had the potted plant war for just one summer before I waved the white flag of surrender and gave up on my deck plants.

Smooch also liked to help with landscaping projects. One of my favorite gardening tools was the Garden Weasel. It was a very meaningful gift from my husband. The first year we celebrated the commercial day of love, he did what a lot of men do. On Valentine's Day, he went to the grocery store and bought crappy roses that would be dead within two days and a funny card about how I steal the bed sheets at night. Now, most women like roses on this day of the year, but not me. Waiting until the last minute and buying the easiest thing he could find was what my dad did for my mom. Completely thoughtless and cheesy. The next year, he did better. I came home to a bright red Garden Weasel complete with a red bow (and no funny card about stealing the bed sheets). That's when I knew he was a keeper. He actually put thought into that gift. He thought about my hobbies and knew the Garden Weasel would help me till areas that needed to be reseeded for grass or prepared for veggies. Every spring, when I got out the Garden Weasel to till the North Carolina red clay soil, Smooch would dance and bark around the tool as I pushed and pulled it over the soil.

Smooch did the same kind of dance with the leaf blower. The first time I used it around her, I playfully aimed it at her large mouth, and her jowls blew open like crazy. Smooch really enjoyed this game and tried to bite the leaf blower each time it was aimed at her. There are still bite marks on the leaf blower that make me chuckle every time I use it. Smooch was a great garden helper in her own special ways.

CHAPTER 27
Pedi-Pedis

WE HAD TO keep Smooch's nails trimmed since she used her giant paws to rake you if you did not give her attention when she wanted it. I tried a local pet grooming place, and they were not a big fan of Smooch. They had me hold her still, backing her into a corner to get to her nails. I gave a nice tip, but the next time I called, they did not have any availability.

My husband had the brilliant idea to file down her nails with a Dremel. This tool was supposed to file down her nails with an ever-so-quiet buzzing sound. Lots of families in our bullmastiff Facebook group raved about the Dremel. But as soon as Smooch heard that buzzing sound, she bolted. Every single time we tried. So much for that pedicure idea.

Next, I tried your basic dog nail clippers. These did not make any sound, so I thought I would have better luck. As soon as I lifted Smooch's paw for a quick nail trim, off she bolted. She would literally hide behind furniture as if we would not be able to see her giant body.

The staff at Companion Camp were the only ones successful in trimming Smooch's nails. They would back her into a corner, slather peanut butter all over her nose, and very quickly snip her nails. We called this procedure Smooch's pedi-pedi, and she got one every time she went to Companion Camp.

CHAPTER 28
Special Sleeping Arrangement

Smooch not only wanted to be by my side during the day, but she also liked for me to sleep with her on the sofa in the living room. You might wonder why we did not let her sleep in our bedroom, which would be a valid question. Well, you see, Smooch got banned in her early years. If she was mad at you for correcting her behavior, she would jump on the bed and pee on it as if to say, "Take that for being mean to me!" Washing a queen-size comforter multiple times a week was not fun, so we put an Invisible Fence flag at the door of the bedroom to indicate this space was off limits.

My husband has terrible insomnia, and if something wakes him up in the middle of the night, he cannot go back to sleep. Smooch figured this out and used it to her advantage. Usually around 1-2 a.m., she would come as close as she could to our bedroom door, slide down on her haunches, and let out a big sigh. Next, she would let out a low, muffled growl, indicating it was time for me to come out and sleep with her. If I did not eject from the bed and come to her, she would let out a deep woof that would wake my husband. So, I learned quickly to listen for the low muffled growl, grab my pillow, and head to the couch. Smooch preferred to sleep next to me so I could rub her chest and back until she fell back to sleep. She would rest her head on the couch, give me a lick on the face, let out a giant sigh, and then lie down next to me. I would stay there until she was fully asleep and snoring loudly. If I left before the snoring started, we would have to repeat the entire process. I literally had a 120-pound toddler for almost seven years.

I also spent some evenings sleeping in the workshop in our backyard. Teenage boy sleepovers can get super loud, so instead of being the mom who yells at them to quiet down and stop jumping like they were going to come through the ceiling, I would grab my pillow and Smooch and head out to sleep on the workshop couch. Smooch loved this arrangement because it meant that I would sleep with her the whole night and not just in the early morning hours.

I did not share these habits with my doctor during my annual physicals. Why? Because I was too embarrassed to admit these behaviors to a professional. Just writing down that a 120-pound dog controlled where and when I slept is embarrassing enough.

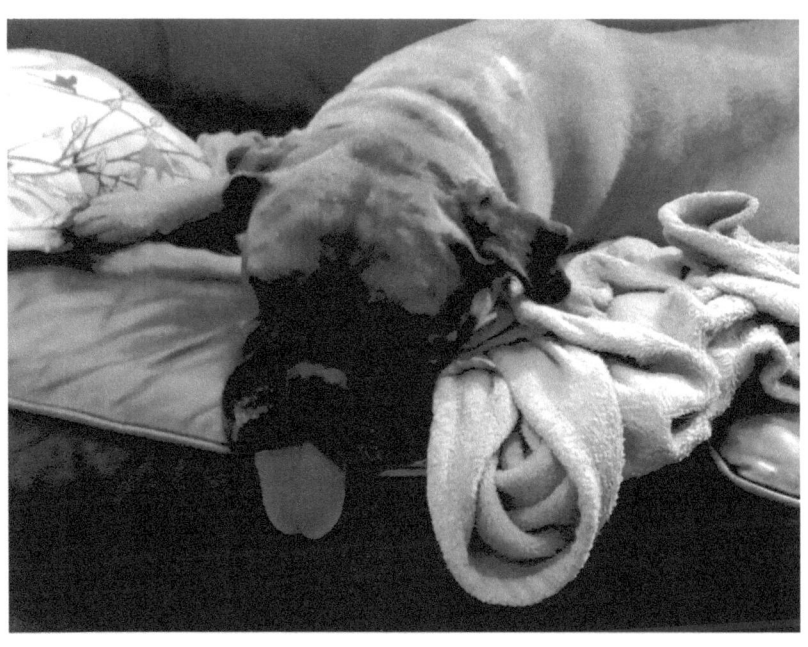

CHAPTER 29
My Last Time with Smooch

FOR SPRING BREAK in 2019, we headed to San Francisco to check off some life bucket list items (think Golden Gate Bridge and Alcatraz). Before we headed out of town, we loaded up all the pets and headed to Companion Camp. We had become good friends with the owners of Companion Camp over the years, and they truly loved our Smooch.

When we arrived for drop-off, a staff member who obviously knew Smooch greeted us. How did I know she knew Smooch? When you arrive at Companion Camp, you are fitted with a plastic collar with your name and cabin number. The staff member greeted Smooch and, pulling out her plastic collar, said, "Oh, Smoochie, you need an extension for your collar, big girl." Yes, our Smooch needed two collars to fit around her giant neck. Smooch trotted to the back office, where they keep the good treats. I called out, "Behave yourself, Smooch, I will see you next Saturday," and I headed home to pack for our trip.

On the Tuesday of our trip, we split up around lunchtime. My husband headed out to lunch with a friend who lives in San Francisco, and the kids and I headed back to our flat for a quick nap. A side note—my husband is affectionately referred to as vacation Clark Griswold. When we travel, he makes sure we see *everything*. We always appreciate him once we are home with all our fun memories, but sometimes certain family members need more downtime than others.

So that Tuesday afternoon, I decided to take a quick nap with my phone ringer turned off. During the nap, my daughter burst into the room and screamed, "Dad is on the phone. Talk to him!" At first, I thought something had happened to him. Then he uttered the three words I could never un-hear. "Smooch is dead."

I was stunned, and I am embarrassed to say my initial question was, "Is this some type of joke?" After all, it was one day after April Fool's Day. Now, I know intellectually that my husband would never make this kind of joke, so why would this be my first question to him? He told me to call Jessica, one of the owners of Companion Camp, but I just couldn't. I did not blame Jessica, but I just could not bring myself to call her. I knew they loved Smooch like one of their own, but for some reason, I could not make that call.

As I was sobbing and sucking in deep breaths, I texted a mutual friend of both Jessica and me. We were not especially close friends, but for some reason, I knew she would understand why I could not breathe or call Jessica. Meredith listened and said all the right things. She is a fellow lover of dogs who are not always easy to love. She asked what she could do to help, and I asked that she coordinate with Jessica to have Smooch's remains cremated. I just could not do it. She asked if we wanted to see Smooch before she was cremated, and I said no instantly, but I asked the rest of the family if they wanted to officially say goodbye. We were all on the same page. We wanted to remember Smooch the way she was the last time we were with her.

Another friend called me as soon as she saw my post on social media. She offered sage advice, as she always does during difficult situations. I swear she was a therapist in a past life. She always had the right words for any trying time. I cannot remember the actual advice she gave that day, but I do remember instantly feeling a sense of calm after talking with her.

My children grieved in very different ways. My son, the cat person, felt guilty for not loving Smooch more. I explained that dogs do not hold grudges and asked if he thought Smooch cared that she was a pain in the ass. He laughed a little and agreed she did not. After all, it was Smooch's world. We just lived in it. My daughter's initial reaction was to not believe it was true. She said she would address it once we were back home.

I spent the next day in our apartment alone, processing it all. My husband took the kids to our scheduled touristy activities while I spent the day looking through pictures of Smooch and writing a blog post in her memory. Smooch was my last baby, my smart and stubborn big girl. I will cherish all the memories I have of her.

CHAPTER 30
The New Normal

COMING HOME WAS hard. Smooch's things were everywhere. My husband offered to get the cats from Companion Camp, and I was grateful for that since I was not sure I could go there yet. He came home with them and Smooch's things, but no Smooch. The staff sent a very sweet card with her things, which included a seed card for us to plant in her memory.

We decided that we needed to put away Smooch's things as soon as we got home. Looking at them made us all sad. I started with her crate. Yes, the almost seven-year-old dog still had a crate. The idea of leaving her to roam freely in the house unsupervised was scary at best. Her crate was in the mudroom, and I am embarrassed to say that area had not been swept or mopped in a long time. And the half-bath connected to it was Smooch's water bowl, so equally unclean. Sweeping up her dog hair and throwing away her half-chewed shoes and dog toys was so very hard.

After coming home, we learned more details of Smooch's death. I had been feeling guilty for going on vacation without her and letting her get chubby and lazy. I was convinced she died because she was too active in the play yard. If I had exercised her more, she would have been in better health and would not have died. My husband learned the details of her death at pickup. Apparently, Smooch trotted out to the dog play yard, looked up, and then fell over. Her heartbeat slowed, then stopped. I try to tell myself that she was happy and pain-free when she died and at a place where she had been happy and loved since she was a puppy. We can all only hope that is the way our life on earth ends.

A friend of mine brought me the most amazing gift that week—a painting of a bullmastiff that she had hanging in her office area. It is the profile of a bullmastiff face, and this particular dog also has a giant tongue. The caption reads, "Life needs more *love*." The letters *love* are Scrabble game pieces. My friend said she thought of Smooch every time she looked at it and that it should be with me now. I cannot think of a more thoughtful gift, and it's an amazing coping mechanism for me. I hung the painting in the hallway next to the master bedroom so I could say good night to Smooch before I headed to bed at night. Friends who are dog people are special, especially during times of grief.

I read Dean Koontz's memoir about his dog Trixie, titled *A Big Little Life: A Memoir of a Joyful Dog Named Trixie*. Below is his explanation of why we give our hearts to dogs. I could not have said it better.

> Dogs' lives are short, too short, but you know that going in. There is going to be loss and great anguish, so you live fully in the moment with her. Never fail to share in her joy, innocence, and delight because you cannot support the illusion that your dog will be your lifelong companion. There is such beauty in the hard honesty of accepting and giving love, knowing it comes with an unbearable price.

The cats were very confused after coming home from Companion Camp. They kept looking around the corners for the beast who desperately wanted to play with them for all these years. After a few days, they started spending more time downstairs in the common areas of the house, which is where Smooch spent most of her time.

My daughter did not appreciate this new arrangement. Our cat Banjo had lived in her room most of the time while Smooch was in our family. And last summer, when she was working through anxiety and depression, Banjo had been there for her like Smooch had for me when my mom died. I had to explain that cats are very different from dogs. Cats love you. I am sure of that. But they are cats in that they put their needs before yours. If more space is open, like a new spot in the sun, then a cat will take that space without question.

Fireball was the exception to this rule. He took on dog-like qualities after Smooch died, sitting next to me while I worked, watched television, and knitted. It was as if he knew I needed him to take over this role as I grieved. I will be forever grateful to Fireball for filling that void after the loss of my Smooch. It was eerie how he knew what I needed, but I accepted the attention with an open heart and arms. Pets really do know how to help their humans.

We also decided to move the litter box and cat dining area downstairs to the mudroom, where Smooch's crate had been. This seemed like a logical solution for the early morning problem my husband had encountered for almost seven years. The cats would meow as soon as he got up for the day. He would explain that there was food upstairs, but the cats would not accept his word. They would meow until he escorted them upstairs to prove that there was, in fact, food in the bowls. Making life a little easier for my husband seemed like a kind thing to do.

Picking up Smooch's ashes was also so very hard. I was struck by how small the container was. How could my big girl fit into that small box? Her body and personality were larger than life. We decided to remember Smooch in a few different ways. I got a memorial necklace to keep some of her ashes close to my heart. We also purchased an urn to keep the majority of her ashes. The urn will live on my work desk, which is pretty much where she was most of the time . . . right next to me. I also kept some ashes to take with me on future lake trips. This way, Smooch is still my lake trip buddy in spirit.

After Smooch's death, I immediately started writing, which is what I do when I am sad or trying to process things. It started with a blog post about losing a pet during the middle-age years, then became this book. I am so grateful for the time I had with my Smooch. She will always be remembered as my last baby.

www.ingramcontent.com/pod-product-compliance
Lightning Source LLC
LaVergne TN
LVHW041623070526
838199LV00052B/3228